WHAT DO WE DO ON ROSH HASHANAH?

Your Fun Picture Guide to Customs, Traditions, and the Meaning of the Jewish New Year

Shira Rose

Copyright

Why this Book?

Hey, kiddos! Let me tell you a little story. So, last year, when Rosh Hashanah rolled around, my own kid—let's call him Little Max—had *a lot* of questions. He heard the shofar and asked, "Mom, is that a magical unicorn horn?" Then he saw the apples and honey and asked, "Wait, are we making dessert out of breakfast now? Where's the rest of the pancake?" And when we went to do Tashlich, he threw the bread into the water and yelled, "Quick, fishies, it's snack time!"

And that's when I realized, kids have the best questions... but I didn't have all the answers. So I thought, "What if there was a super fun book that explained everything in a way that *actually* makes sense to kids?" A book that answers all the big, funny, and sometimes wacky questions you've got about Rosh Hashanah!

That's how this book came to life. It's full of silly stories, cool facts, and even some fun activities that will help you figure out things like why we eat apples and honey (no, it's not because bees are invited to dinner), why we blow a shofar (nope, not to start a marching band), and why we throw bread into the water (don't worry, the fish won't get full).

So, if you're anything like Little Max and want to know all about Rosh Hashanah while having a good laugh, this is the book for you! Let's make this Rosh Hashanah the most fun and interesting one yet. Ready to dive in? Trust me, the fish are waiting!

Introduction

Hey there, little adventurer! Ready to go on a journey to learn about one of the coolest holidays ever? It's called Rosh Hashanah (yeah, it's a mouthful, but you'll get used to it!). So, what's it all about, you ask?

Well, imagine a giant party that lasts two days! But it's not just any party—it's the **Jewish New Year**. Nope, not the one with fireworks and funny glasses (though that sounds fun too). This is a special kind of new year where we get to look back on the past year, say, "Oops! I'll try to do better next time," and then look forward to an awesome, fresh start!

Rosh Hashanah is like hitting the reset button on a video game—except this time, you're the hero of your own story. You get to think about all the amazing things you'll do in the new year, eat sweet treats like apples dipped in honey (yum!), and hear the loudest, craziest sound ever—the shofar! (That's a big horn, and trust me, it's loud enough to wake up the neighborhood squirrels.)

So, why do we celebrate it? Because it's all about becoming the best YOU. And hey, who doesn't love a holiday where you get to blow a horn, eat yummy food, and get a fresh start? Let's dive in and learn all the fun stuff we do on Rosh Hashanah. Are you ready? Let's go!

Why Do We Celebrate Rosh Hashanah?

Why do we celebrate Rosh Hashanah? Is it because we love apples and honey? Well, yes, but there's more to it than just yummy treats (although that part is awesome)!

Rosh Hashanah is like the world's coolest **New Year's party**. But instead of just shouting "Happy New Year!" and watching fireworks, we use this time to think about the *big* stuff. Think of it like this: imagine if you had a magic mirror that lets you look back at everything you did last year. Some of it was super cool, right? But maybe some things could've been better, like sharing your toys or helping with the dishes.

Rosh Hashanah gives us the chance to say, "Hey, this is my moment to be even better next year!" It's all about **reflection**, which is just a fancy way of saying we think about what we've done and how we can make the new year even more awesome!

It's also a time for **renewal**, which means starting fresh—like a superhero getting a new costume and superpowers. You get to think, "What kind of hero do I want to be this year? Maybe one who helps more, laughs more, and does cool stuff to make the world a better place!"

BA'AL TOKE'A
( )

The Shofar

Alright, kiddos! Let me introduce you to the star of the Rosh Hashanah show: the *Shofar*! Now, this isn't just any horn—it's a super special one made from a ram's horn (yup, that's right, from a real ram). And boy, is it loud! The kind of loud that could wake up the whole neighborhood, including your dog.

But why do we blow the Shofar? Well, the Shofar is like a big, echoing alarm clock for our hearts and minds. When we hear it, it's saying, "Hey! It's time to wake up! Time to be our best selves!" It's a call to think about what we've done this past year and what we can do better in the new one.

The sound of the Shofar reminds us to *pay attention*—not to math class or chores, but to the things that really matter. It's like the ultimate superhero horn, calling us to action! It tells us to reflect, be brave, and get ready for a fresh start.

Apples and Honey

Alright, my sweet little friends, let's talk about one of the *yummiest* parts of Rosh Hashanah—**apples and honey**! Now, this isn't just a snack we eat because it's super tasty (though it really is!). Apples dipped in honey are a *symbol* of what we want for the new year—a year full of sweetness, joy, and all the good stuff you can think of!

So, why apples? Well, apples are juicy and delicious, just like we hope the new year will be. They're a classic, just like Rosh Hashanah traditions. And why honey? Because it's sticky, sweet, and oh-so-delicious, just like we want our year to stick with happiness and sweetness from start to finish.

When we take a bite of that apple dripping with honey, we're basically saying, "Hey, new year, bring it on! Make this one as sweet as can be!"

Family Traditions on Rosh Hashanah

Okay, little ones, let's take a peek into how families celebrate Rosh Hashanah all around the world! This holiday is all about bringing everyone together— moms, dads, grandparents, cousins, and even the family dog (if they're lucky enough to grab a taste of the apples and honey).

One of the best parts of Rosh Hashanah is the **festive meal**! Imagine a big, beautiful table covered with yummy foods—round challah bread (so fluffy and delicious), apples dipped in honey, pomegranates bursting with seeds (each seed is like a little wish for the new year!), and other special treats that make this meal super fun. Everyone gathers around to eat, share stories, and laugh together.

But wait, there's more! Before we dig into all that tasty food, families say **blessings and prayers** to give thanks and hope for a sweet and happy year ahead. It's a time to reflect, say nice things about each other, and maybe even share what you hope to do in the coming year—like being extra kind, or finally cleaning your room without being asked!

Different families have different ways of celebrating. Some sing traditional songs, some tell stories about Rosh Hashanah from long ago, and some even go outside to do **Tashlich** (remember, that's when we toss bread into the water to say goodbye to mistakes from the past year).

No matter how families celebrate, one thing is for sure—Rosh Hashanah is a time for **togetherness**, sweetness, and lots of love. So, what's your favorite part of celebrating with your family?

Write your Favorite Part of Celebrating with Your Family?

Tashlich

Alright, little adventurers, let's talk about one of the coolest Rosh Hashanah traditions—**Tashlich**! Imagine standing by a river or a lake with a piece of bread in your hand. Now, that bread isn't for feeding the ducks (though they might think so), it's for something super special.

Tashlich is all about saying goodbye to mistakes we made over the past year. It's like hitting the *delete* button on things you're not so proud of, like when you didn't share your toys or forgot to clean up your room. We take small pieces of bread, and as we toss them into the water, we're symbolically "casting away" those mistakes. Goodbye, mistakes—hello, fresh start!

It's a time to reflect on how we can be kinder, braver, and even more awesome in the new year. And hey, watching the bread float away is kind of fun too, like your mistakes are literally drifting out of sight!

Reflection and Prayer

Alright, little thinkers! Now that we've talked about all the fun and tasty stuff, it's time for one of the most important parts of Rosh Hashanah— **reflection and prayer**. Think of it like looking in a magic mirror and seeing all the things you did this past year. Some things might make you smile, like when you helped a friend or shared your toys. But maybe there are other things you'd like to change, like the time you didn't listen or forgot to clean your room (uh-oh!).

Reflection is when we think about those things and ask ourselves, "How can I be better in the new year?" It's a time to say, "Oops, I'll try harder next time," and make promises to be even more awesome next year. This is also when we say special **prayers** to ask for help in making the new year full of kindness, laughter, and success!

And just like when you make a superhero plan to save the day, this is the time to plan out all the good things you'll do in the year ahead. It's your chance to start fresh and move forward with *big dreams* and *good deeds*!

Interactive Section for Rosh Hashanah in the Synagogue

Now, this is where YOU come in! Grab a pencil or crayon and think about this: What's one thing you want to get better at in the new year? Is it being kinder to your friends? Maybe helping out more at home? Or perhaps it's learning something new and exciting? Write down something special that you want to work on for the coming year, and let it remind you of all the awesome things you're going to accomplish!

Rosh Hashanah in the Synagogue

Alright, kiddos! Now, let's take a trip to the synagogue during Rosh Hashanah. This is where some of the most important and special moments of the holiday happen! When families gather together in the synagogue, it's all about **prayers, blessings, and readings** that help us start the new year right.

First off, the synagogue is filled with people dressed in their best clothes, excited for the new year ahead. You'll hear beautiful, peaceful **prayers** that talk about kindness, forgiveness, and making the world a better place. It's a time to reflect on the past year and ask for help to be even better in the coming year.

There are also special **readings** from the Torah (which is like the superhero storybook of Jewish teachings!). These readings remind us of the lessons we've learned and the ones we still need to work on. It's like getting the ultimate pep talk for the year ahead.

But here's the fun part—the **Shofar** gets blown! Remember that big, curly horn we talked about? When it blasts, it fills the room with its loud, exciting sound, waking everyone up to the important work of starting fresh and reflecting.

It's a big moment, and it's one that makes you feel proud to be part of something special.

How to Get Ready for Rosh Hashanah

Alright, kiddos, it's almost time for Rosh Hashanah, and you know what that means—it's time to get ready! But how do we prepare for this special holiday? Let's find out!

1. **Baking the Challah**: First up, it's time to make the challah. But not just any challah— on Rosh Hashanah, the challah is round to represent the circle of life and the endless possibilities of the new year. You can help by rolling the dough and watching it bake into a big, golden loaf!

2. **Setting the Table**: Next, we get the table ready. It's time to bring out the fancy dishes and set the table with everything we'll need for the festive meal. Don't forget the apples, honey, pomegranates, and, of course, the challah!

3. **Decorating the House**: You can make your house extra special by adding fun decorations like candles, flowers, or even drawings you make! This helps set the mood for a sweet, joyful new year.

4. **Preparing the Prayers**: Get your prayer books ready for all the special blessings and prayers that are part of the Rosh Hashanah celebration. It's a time to reflect, be thankful, and ask for a great new year ahead!

5. **Getting Ready for Tashlich**: Don't forget to gather some bread crumbs for Tashlich, where we cast away our past mistakes into the water. It's a fun and meaningful way to start the year fresh!

Setting Goals for the New Year

Hey there, future goal-setters! Now that Rosh Hashanah is here, it's the perfect time to think about all the amazing things you want to do in the year ahead. Setting goals is kind of like planting seeds in a garden—you take care of them, and soon enough, they grow into something incredible!

What are some goals you can think about? Maybe it's about being kinder to your friends, learning something new like riding a bike or playing an instrument, or even helping more around the house (bonus points for extra hugs to mom and dad!). No matter how big or small, your goals are like little promises to yourself that you'll make this year the best one yet!

And here's the best part: your goals are *yours*—no one else can choose them for you. So take a moment to think about what matters most to you and how you want to grow, explore, and have fun this year!

Setting Goals for the New Year

Hey there, future goal-setters! Now that Rosh Hashanah is here, it's the perfect time to think about all the amazing things you want to do in the year ahead. Setting goals is kind of like planting seeds in a garden—you take care of them, and soon enough, they grow into something incredible!

What are some goals you can think about? Maybe it's about being kinder to your friends, learning something new like riding a bike or playing an instrument, or even helping more around the house (bonus points for extra hugs to mom and dad!). No matter how big or small, your goals are like little promises to yourself that you'll make this year the best one yet!

And here's the best part: your goals are *yours*—no one else can choose them for you. So take a moment to think about what matters most to you and how you want to grow, explore, and have fun this year!

Interactive Element

This is where YOU get to shine! In the space below, write something special you want to accomplish in the new year. It could be anything—

from becoming a better artist to reading more books or even being a better friend. Whatever you choose, this is your chance to make the year ahead extra awesome!

Closing Thoughts

Wow! What an exciting journey we've been on together, learning all about Rosh Hashanah! ☐ We've talked about delicious apples and honey, the big blast of the shofar, special moments with family, and even how we can cast away our mistakes with Tashlich. But there's one last thing to think about before we wrap up this adventure: **What does Rosh Hashanah mean to YOU?**

Rosh Hashanah isn't just about the food or the fun traditions (though they are pretty awesome!). It's about something much bigger. It's about thinking of ways to make the world a little better each day—by being kind, helpful, and brave. It's also a time to look at all the things we've done in the past and get excited about what's coming next.

As we say goodbye to last year and welcome the new year, think about what you've learned and how you can use those lessons to become an even more amazing YOU. Whether it's being kinder to others, working hard on your goals, or just spreading joy with your big, bright smile —everything you do helps make the world a better place.

So, as you celebrate Rosh Hashanah this year, remember that it's not just a holiday—it's a **fresh start**, a time to reflect, and a chance to grow into the best version of yourself. Carry those lessons with you throughout the year, and no matter what, know that you're always moving forward with a heart full of hope and sweetness.

Write a reflection on what the holiday means and how you can carry its lessons throughout the year...

Made in the USA
Las Vegas, NV
20 September 2024

95567301R00026